HERE ON EARTH

Jeffrey Wainwright was born in Stoke-on-Trent, educated locally and at Leeds University where he benefited from the poetry scene sustained by Jon Silkin, Ken Smith, Geoffrey Hill and others. He taught for many years at Manchester Metropolitan University. He has also translated drama (from French) and his critical prose includes *Poetry the Basics* and *Acceptable Words: Essays on the Poetry of Geoffrey Hill*. This is his ninth volume of poetry, all published by Carcanet. He lives with his wife in Manchester and for parts of the year in Umbria and New South Wales.

Here on Earth

JEFFREY WAINWRIGHT

CARCANET POETRY

First published in Great Britain in 2022 by
Carcanet
Alliance House, 30 Cross Street
Manchester, M2 7AQ
www.carcanet.co.uk

A CIP catalogue record for this book is
available from the British Library.

ISBN 978 1 80017 275 3

Book design by Andrew Latimer
Printed in Great Britain by SRP Ltd, Exeter, Devon

The publisher acknowledges financial
assistance from Arts Council England.

CONTENTS

for Judith

HERE I COME

Here I come, as though
down a water-slide, head-first
from my mother's crying,
shouldering her pelvic bone, mucus-clad,
bloodied, slithering, hard to grasp,
gulping at this foreign gas,
screwed-up against the light.
Here is all there is of me,
me exactly,
into life and clinging to it
without reflection, the boundary of me,
the knuckle, kneecap,
anything there is to celebrate,
anything divine,
is here in this wawl, squirm and slather.

THE DAY BEGINS

They come into my room, these friends
whom I am always glad to see,
and insist that it is past dawn,
time to get up now.
They are bright and positive
and I am happy to hear this news
for here, lying on my back, I have been waiting
and it means I have come through.
They busy themselves about the room,
tidying, preparing,
bumping at the edges of my dream.
They are so trustworthy these friends
why would I not get up and taste the day?

NATURE NOTES

from a train:

two crows gleaning a shaven field

some dozen naked sheep nearby

I have nothing else to say on this

##

a scuffling in the undergrowth:
something wants to live unseen,
to escape notice, to make good

##

along the woodland path
this full tangle of youthful trees,
creepers, white flowers

a blotch of orange springing
from a long-fallen tree

##

its body stamped into the gravel
half-way down, printed by a tyre-track
the snake's head is intact,
its mouth open, stricken

it must have lived on like this

##

I am paused by a cobweb in the climbing-rose,
only seen in a sudden light,
awaiting the blunderers

near the light
lies the information,
the cunning architecture
of each voracious thread

##

a young fox in the headlights
turns back across the road -
the wrong choice
but it makes it

##

the yucca flowers late
its white compilations look fleecy from here
those sharp green leaves
its ramparts

on it goes

##

peaceable this whole scene
odd plots of vines, olives.
fingers of forestry, some pasture

in gray light it seems doleful
but no, leave all that behind,
just look: every single shoot intent

##

flies, specks, beetles clambering expertly
across a table or a tree
a bee heedless of its hum
a butterfly -
what can summarise all this?

##

birds of every stripe, even if at war
one with another, busy themselves
with life, will take a crumb that's offered
or leave it,
they will use our buildings
if amenable, our nooks and eaves,
our high places, but still keep their own life,
themselves to themselves,
their strange songs also constant

##

ivy dominating this patch of ground,
a thorny stick, a tree stump
flaking to pieces but fecund,
the fungi now in their season,
their pristine caps suddenly there,
brown oak-leaves among the litter,
two pale stones, a small cluster of cyclamen
all purple together

##

a vixen
(as I think)
takes her ease
in the soft dusk
close to lights

ready
but quite unhurried
even though
this is a human lawn

##

these poor leaves shaken off

once moist, rolled tight in expectation,
now crêpe beneath their tree

everything is in alteration

a pair of trousers   an arthritic thumb

DISILLUSIONMENT

rain glints on the copper beech
standard cirrus motionless above

that will do –
the poem has been here
or hereabouts
many times
and what does it do
with its words?
where does it take us to?

are these rain glints
the very ones I think I saw?

disillusionment can fall
at any hour
nine eleven or twelve
just as words do
in or out of poems

remorseless
their pitter-patter

LANDSCAPE

(I)

It is not to the landscape the sadness belongs.
That is folded, mostly as we would wish,
and is steady and companionate,
its trees sheltering the special field,
that track right-angled to suit our will.
Yet sadness is part of it and so must come
from some presumption that is ours alone,
some arrogation that we depend upon.
How patiently the landscape stays with us.
Can it know how vulnerable we are?

(II)

It is a consolation for us this pleated
and slightly savage land, that and its crowded sky.
It can be claimed to be a friend, almost
as though it could converse through its clefts,
harmonise its fractured songs
and listen via the branches of its modest trees.
The harder truth is that it pays no such attention;
shelter or shade are an accidental benison.
Is there any way we can convince ourselves
that we are not ignored among the grass and stars?

(III)

I feel I have to blame the scene at large:
dark matter, distant dust, fruitful asteroids –
time – although it can no more be sensible
than any of the flowers it will not own.
It stands apart from joy and is unimpressed.
And this is why I resent its safe indifference:
how can it hold a kind of life such as
these successful shoots, water that cannot be stilled
and care for none of it at all?   ('Care'
a word we have found for ourselves hereabouts.)

(IV)

What am I saying here?   Do I imply
that because there is so much around us
sturdily independent of anything we can think
or feel, there should be no cause for grief?
How small we are against approaching stars,
even against the potent busyness of worms.
Why must we want all this context
to validate us, to feel admitted by
the great unconsciousness of moss,
halting rivulets, windblown straw?

A BATCH OF FRAIL FLOWERS

a batch of frail flowers, a purplish pink,
hang close to the shadowed grass

there they are, yes just there, frail
flowers of a purplish pink

do you see that, and what do you see?
and 'shadowed grass', what do you make of that?

you might suppose it is close to dusk
as I write, though equally you might suspect
I'm clawing at consequence,
something to make the frail flowers last
into wherever they now find themselves

suddenly adjacent to thistledown
bumping against the window-pane

WALKING IN THE RAIN

Why would I go walking in the rain?
There is some gleam on surfaces
but not much for the light is faint.
The fallen leaves, lemonish and dull bronze,
cling together once gathered by the wind.
But what am I doing?
inviting melancholy, something close to solitude?
I must buy a loaf on the way home,
glad to have a project offered.

A RECTANGULAR GARDEN

At the upper right-hand corner
a large vase, terra cotta, but not an amphora,
and, just by, a palm-bush, its narrow, sharp leaves
like a comb, some of them yellow to the end,
the higher ones still a heavy green;
then, stretching along the edge, seven or eight
large stones embedded lengthways to make a border,
one pink flower remaining on the bushes there;
and I arrive at the next corner,
a grey wall of painted breezeblock,
a gap of light between every two blocks,
in fact the wall is castellated for rough effect;
light also falls on a thorn creeper that has escaped
the dense bushes clustered at the foot
of the mighty tree which is the glory of the scene;
a thin vine, whose flowers hang like catkins
about the length and colour of candles,
more than survives as it clutches the thorn,
breaking wave-like over it, winding and grasping;
where it has yet to reach the thorn-flower,
those blooms, copious and defiant pink,
look to survive deep into autumn;
coming along the third side a wooden fence,
here and there slightly mossed, some grass
pushing at the battens and planks
and two herb plots, now mostly desolate
save for some sage, parsley and tarragon,
all mis-labelled; a tap fastened to a wooden post
looks little used but ready;

this is the fourth side, the terrace bricks from which
I see all this, the curled leaves scattered
about the lawn, the upturned table I missed
in the bottom corner, its feet of gnarled and rusty iron.

~

On the paving, before the garden proper, a large
terra-cotta vase, quite empty, and behind it
a wooden fence, two metres high, and saplings
that will grow no higher, drawn up in tight array,
beside a palm, also limited, its yellowing leaves
bending earthwards; the flower-bed holds
perhaps a dozen flowers, roses possibly, all the way
to the first corner where an upturned table
lies abandoned beside a breezeblock wall,
some iron fencing a further boundary;
the tree, grand, grandiloquent even, brawny,
its bark roughcast yet still elegant, reaches
and spreads its own proportion over the garden's
leaf-strewn lawn, the tumble of bushes
that cover the wall and bound the bottom edge,
the deep pink bougainvillea, as I have learned
it is called since my previous turn, offers
great dishes of flower to a black and white butterfly
out at work; then the third side is nondescript,
just a fence against next door, a dry standpipe,
its hose looped loosely across the grass,
two herb beds enclosed by wood,
grasses rearing up the sides as though to peer
at a parsley plant, the beginnings of a sage bush
and some tarragon, fending off the weeds;

here on the bricks on the fourth side
a low divan and some cushions, still damp
from the morning rain, a straggling petunia,
its brave red flowers optimistic beneath my chair
from where there's so much to be seen:

~

The large vase, terra-cotta, but not an amphora...

PARMENIDES ON THE BOARDWALK

Out on the boardwalk today for another 'health walk'.
It keeps our feet out of the watery ground.
As usual I stop by the tree-stump decorated
with a fungus nicely confined between
splits in the wood and the curve of the bark.
A terrier passes by, as eager as ever.
Today the fungus is the pale green of a paint-chart
and is hard to the touch, plaster-like, resistant.
Is it dried and dead or in yet another phase?
If dead what was the life that has been lost?

No matter there is life everywhere,
energy in every form.
Velvet mosses clothe the bark of fallen trees;
turn up a log and shiny grubs protest at the light;
in the turbid pools the hog-louse nudges past
the ravenous nymphs of the damsel fly –
the beautiful demoiselle; leaves gleam freshly
in the reviving undergrowth; garlic
awaits its flowers; blackthorn vaunts its snowy clouds;
bacteria will be hereabouts striving furiously
as they do in yoghourt and in sourdough,
simple souls but hard as nails, their plasmids
and their daughter cells, their flagellas,
some of them, beating always towards the light.
All this comes by book or the information board
we also use to spot a bulky thrush, a robin
or that pert and fussy wren – are their 'songs'
as material as a ribosome?   Another question.

Look, is that Parmenides, sandalled as we might expect,
avoiding a springer on a too-long lead?
He's valuing sense enough here,
a trip or fall would interrupt philosophy.
Further down the boardwalk that must be his goddess
waiting to accost him once again.   Her cagoule is perfect.
I edge closer to listen in to what she says.
She seems to think Parmenides needs a refresher
on the One since Plato dragged it to his cave
and made of it a fashionable Idea or Form
not something solid like the ribosome.
Others, she warns, are so in thrall to the jazzy tumult
of the world they think that Reason is capsized
and Truth a mirage or a fantasy.

Poor Parmenides, you're going to have a job
getting that into your old hexameters.
Is what she's saying that the hog-louse, damsel
and bacterium are not a numbered aggregate
of different things but share something
that makes them shift and scurry, predators
and prey, and that makes them One, and us One
with them as we seize our breakfast for another day?

Parmenides shivers in the vexatious English breeze
and comes back along the boardwalk.
He nods and that gives me the nerve to speak to him.
This One, I say, *is an idea I like*
though I'm not sure why – it might be Truth.
I know it's simpler to see gnats swarming
to no tune at all, or starlings as merely particular
and not try to seek the rhyme or reason
of their gatherings.   I hope you are going to set me straight.
He puffs his cheeks and makes as though to speak

but then steps off the boardwalk, taking care
where he puts his foot, and disappears.
I walk on, sidling past a mastiff across the path
alert and listening for its owner's call.
The trees resume their patient climb,
the small dishes of fungus … no - too much to itemise.
The thought-filled sky absorbs it all.
I'm looking for an ending where the cadence falls.

FIRE-SMOKE

How slow this fire-smoke rising from the field.
It saunters upwards wholly at leisure
relinquishing itself contentedly enough.

This is now a morning in deep autumn,
the last leaves going but no longer plunging down,
the lights are on, the trees resolutely black
against this ancient wash-water sky.

Where is the burden here? But why translate
what comes to the eye already changed?
They did not stand a chance – 'ancient' and 'at leisure' –
they were enrolled as soon as glimpsed.

THE LUCKY TREE

To survive the winter ice the lucky tree
whose lucky seed found a post
in sympathetic ground still work
along its column's reach, draw down
into its roots all moisture and nutrition,
surrendering its leaves to the year's entropy.
The whole tree must live, its patient leaves
must flutter into death, part of the system
which we see as cruel abandonment -
Ah, the fond complacencies of metaphor!

TREES FALLING

Trees fall, of course they do,
not quite as we are taken,
but something like,
cognate, similar.

This is a verse that pleases me
but not its import:
that trees have an end
and that we follow.

So roll up your canvas rug,
imagine nothing stronger,
imagine nothing stronger than
what will fall at last.

Pack only certain clothes,
leave the rest behind.
'Rest' will prove a word
welcome eventually.

And is 'fall' another such?
(*vide* the trees above)
every kind of rug,
words on their own parade.

STANDARD MODEL

So here we find ourselves, for now,
deep in the Standard Model,
that is the way the universe is lawfully arranged
from a toilet brush to neutrinos,
though the smaller things get
the more doubtful they become,
at best a momentary smear across a screen
– was it there at all, and what does that mean?
And they, these bosons and fermions,
are everywhere, even beyond the next galaxy
and pass through everything
like a ghost through a wall –
anything but standard.
The sun on my arm, noticed briefly,
the smell of ragwort, torn and rent,
everything we are aware of
inside and outside our words
may have its bedrock in these bosons and their like
keeping us and telling us we are alive.

HERE ON EARTH

1

Dear Adolfo, whose joy everyday was this panorama
and your cabin in the woods
where the world was all yours, what cruelty
could make you leave it all?   Salad leaves, mint,
tomatoes, sunny zucchini flowers,
strange clefted herbs, these were your province,
your own space and time
your own angolo *in which the universe*
becomes its proper size, your kitchen,
your simple garden plot, your rifugio.

2

Birds have a place in the wilderness of stars.
One alights, lurching on a branch until
it can change motion into balance,
the key to its life, just as a planet holds its steady roll.
And nearby, microbes, bacteria and other
smallest things live out their purposes
gifted from that strange fission long ago,
its bits now swirling outwards from nowhere
and cooling as gently as a bird
despite its striving to stay warm and alive.

3

The tree's slow climb is probably complete,
this is its customary canopy,
its lowest branches heavy to the ground.
Coppery its leaves, that was decided long ago
in whatever variation gave them
an advantage to intersperse regulation
avenues of dutiful poplars perfect
for guards of honour, though what came first,
the love of medals, lanyards, bayonets
or natural shuffling towards what's best?

4

The cicadas round here choose 11.30
to begin their daily chaunt, or whistle,
or clatter or whatever words have evolved
to suit their translation to our different codes.
Less than ten minutes and they quiet once more.
Perhaps the heat fails them as the breeze
disturbs whatever governs their antique limbs.
Time, moving air, the sun's warmth
might form the concert governing
the cicadas' call, utterance, rattle.

5

Grasshopper, locust, a lizard fallen
into a water pail are all part of what began
some time ago and it is their various deaths
that stipulate intervals, clock-time
and which things come last. And such
feelings as these are must have come
of what we know was rock, magma,
anyway insensate stuff. The ant's forefoot
has been seen as salvational,
such is the import of a dab of DNA.

6

The mouse escapes, out of the door, up the path
then darts left for cover, a major event
in its biography this encounter
with the human giants.
Its life is clandestine, nocturnal, bent
upon avoidance, governed by useful fear.
To us it seems no kind of life
but it shows no sign of resignation
or subservience to the wall of fate.
It has escaped and will look to flee next time.

7

This dry cistern and this tankard are 'full of life',
much of it microbial it is true
and of the kind trapped in aspic or in ice
or in Bartleby's prison yard, and all of it,
like this red speck voyaging across my page,
purposeful.   Could this have been predicted?
If so when?   When all was 'matter', nothing more
– scientists can find no better word –
and 'when' does not seem so useful at this distance.
My red speck has gone.   It will be living somewhere.

8

Above and below, birds and fish, none of them
earthbound, ever seem to trudge
though sometimes life must feel hard –
however it was invented life *is* hard,
for elephants who must cross China,
for widows, for children by a broken water-pump.
A bowl of cherries, not!   The habits of syntax
bring us to expound the counter-claim:
the sun with his hat on …his own side of the street
though it is in fact dying, no ifs or buts.

9

Life was this small leaf, detached by happenstance,
curled, yellow now overwhelming its atolls
of green.   Poor leaf how I pity you.
You are only of interest now as mulch,
no more springing, no more riffling with the wind
your fond but faithless partner.   But –
that word always returns eventually –
wet mulch, a company of leaves,
will keep water in the soil meaning
a succession of leaves and more life.

10

Out there, in the 'vast rondures', light
and it seems naught else.   No matter,
here we have enough to be going on with.
Look at it all! The usual ants
teeming and bustling on the subway steps,
a single snake in a hole.
What accountancy can adumbrate
a herd of deer on even one estate?
Out of what we can call nothing, all this!
and the snake giving birth in its hole.

11

Flowers are a popular sort of life,
those pinks advertising their solid shoots,
small roses, gaura riding the breeze
on their slender stems as though enjoying
their jeopardy, calling in the insects
to their tiny stars, a neat reciprocity
with the busy fly, and celandines
cushioned in the grass, their buttery yellow
belying their modesty.   How we love the characters
we make of them besides the beauty of their souls.

12

Geology and gravity are here to show us where we are.
Imagine oceans falling from the basins
where they lie out into nothingness.
Imagine our little earth without its atmosphere,
no longer a handsome globe, quite contained,
but grey and knobbly, chamfered nowhere
save for the blinding salt flats, perhaps
a desert here or there.   That is how it was
and the rocks strewn everywhere preserve
our history in the impress of a fern.

13

Can we count ourselves amongst the wonders of the universe?
We understand that there is a universe,
a sun and suns, stars far off from here
and how it is all molecular.
We nearly understand ourselves, not just
how to build a nest or den
but how to govern our multitudes, combat
our sicknesses, at least to within tolerances
we can accept.   And the big idea:
we shall have no need of tolerances, everything will fit.

14

Or might we be an offcut or grit from
the passing gale of the universal matter
on its way to nowhere leaving us
to repine on this fretful isle, its bird-calls
the model of our own anxiety.
They call to their own, much as we are left
to do since we have realised the vacancy
about us. The wreckage that has formed
our mother earth has done well to take us
out of magma and of fire but could not sidestep...

15

To put it simply, why is there …?
Why does everything cool, as an act of nature,
A brawny ingot and a dish of tea?
What is happening to all those pieces
that left us long ago?   Are they discovering
oxygen or something else that can stamp
the beginnings of what we would recognise
as life, some familiar lichen, but this time
with a permanent inscription in its cells
that forbids what we know as… death.

16

Undeniably this is a wonderful world!
For a bit broken off, graphite, dull carbon,
it has bloomed as we live it now,
convenient, congenial, hospitable even,
oxygen somehow out of light, photo-
synthesis, and so, as Joseph Priestley said,
'no vegetable grows in vain'. The humble
fennel bulb, the various beans all continue
and we have something to look forward to
besides, content in the corner, Bosco the dog.

17

Apricots weaken and fall into the roadway.
They have done their job but will get
no purchase in the pounded dust
nor in the seams of paving stones.
Specks, birds and wasps, as well as us
benefit from this excess, this year anyway,
and in this part of the zone where the frost
did not claw the flowers. Is there a law,
forged deep in a capsule of the fission flare,
applying itself to this chosen tree?

18

We strive to make things beautiful,
a finial over a gateway, jasmine's
white stars climbing. We are convinced all this
will enhance the known brevity of our stay,
in some instances not only occupy but define
the time, sometimes with nature's say-so,
even with a willing partnership.
Much beauty will outlive us which is why
we press seeds into gaps and crevices.
Rock alone can never be enough.

19

Things come to seem strange as our time goes by.
This abbey for instance, its uneven stones
perfectly dressed, is enclosed now with
a kitchen-garden and a patch of vines.   Beneath
the perfect proportion of campanile and church
are said to lie the bones of Syrian monks
who first brought the Word west
to Roman Umbria.   Somewhere they lie,
probably in no order.   What is East and West?
The compass needle shivers and tries to stop.

20

However well-chosen the spot it still makes sense
to recognise us in the knockings from
 a cold tobacco-pipe, not much different
in make-up – just the matter, clinker
and common ash to be readily resumed,
drawn back into the firmament
with planets, some accelerating stars
and loose matter. Our mighty consciousness,
less than a raindrop in this company,
clings to 'mean' among its desperate words.

21

Must we celebrate this surprising globe?
It seems given to us that we should,
especially now that the blue-white entity,
seen from outside seems no more than a zephyr
curling round, drawing us to its share
of gravid force.   For some, for many, for most
they find that neither grass nor gravity
is congenial.   The earth has performed its tasks,
ground obdurate stuff down to silken sand,
but still there are lacks it cannot remedy.

22

Grinding is the motion that is most advanced,
mountain against mountain, the slow granulation
whether tempest or earthquake have worn
a cornice into pumice or to sand. We seize its use,
melt sand towards the most translucent glass,
talc quarried to dust a new child's skin –
nothing could be further from the granite face.
And could that be the end of us as the last bone
finds its way into a shovelful of silica
and that into a sandstorm or moveable dust?

23

This is a place where nothing grows.   Nothing.
It is just a coastal sweep of sand,
empty shipwrecks, empty wind squalls.
Not a beetle climbs out of the sand,
no plasmid gets busy here or even stretches itself.
Is this how it will end or how it did begin?
Will the heat hereabouts shrivel into darkness
like a leaf drying and changing colour,
the only thing left that can change
cooling steadily towards the absolute?

24

The luck to lie out on meadow or on lawn,
absorb the mildest sun, is surely with us,
granted by the unsteady earth in its moments
of repose. With luck too we avoid
its angry shrugs, volcano, flood, tempest,
drought though these might have proved
the one condition chosen for our post.
Unless it can be shown that it is not luck
but our curacy has softened this rock
enough to bring a welcome harvest home.

25

The velvet three-note ring-dove's call
towards some other bird, is it anxious
or content?   Whichever, it has its place
in the catalogue of cries, the shriek
as the owl takes its prey, the recognition
as the long-lost fulmar finds its home.
All these have been worked out, barks and cries,
suited to how they manage in this special world.
They stumble singly but still keep their kind
apprised of how to live at least for now.

26

It is easy to see this globe as a trundling
bowling-ball, nothing graceful, elegant
or light, rather a cruel rock
misshapen, palsied, its tough lianas
catching at the foot, its gales forcing us
to ground, breaking roof-trees, razing dikes,
its bilious water stretching to the sea,
its plagues finding the perfect host,
nothing discomfited to require a death
for a death, in fact requiring nothing.

PIECES OF COAL

New Year

just now
on New Year's Eve
I could not source
a lump of coal

2020 has no use
for such stuff
not even a fist-sized
chunk of the kind
that might once
have been picked
off the pit-heap
by a nine-year-old
kept off school.

a hundred years ago it got everywhere
the home-fires of Berlin
the locomotives by the Nile
Lisbon's town gas
Sweden's ironworks
the abbatoirs of Argentina
our coal
our good luck
that we could ship it
so easy to the sea
and everywhere at home
a load tipped in the entry
as the collier's ration
shovelled into fireboxes
across the nation

briquettes lit
by a gas poker
(coal gas of course)
and in fifty years
it is nowhere
finger-nails and town halls
are scrubbed clean
tips greened
into leisure walks
the coalhouse
now storage for any old thing

a piece of coal
a metonym
for fuel,
for food
for warmth
and how we need that
as the first-footer knows
from his five minutes
in the cold –
who's a lucky lad?

Florence

A million-tonner
the year it was shut,
Florence pit stood
at the end of our street.
I never knew
that it was named
for this solemn, aristocratic girl,
–daughter of the third duke –

though it was he who labelled
the whole neighbourhood,
Lennox, Hamilton, Buccleuch, Rothesay
as well as Florence Primary
with its stubby tower,
slightly Italianate,
a totem for the stolid terraces,
Leveson, Gower, Blantyre and St Clair.

Nowhere in her fixes
of albumen and silver
does Florence look content.
The white cat in her lap
probably more a prop
than a pet,
the watercolour retriever
only a temporary friend.
Not for her to guest
as a gutsy Coal Queen
at the miners' picnic,
she was dead at twenty-six
of her third childbed,
a bloody mess no doubt,
not unlike the accidental agony
by then familiar
in her father's chambers
deep below
the doomed pilasters
of Barry's Trentham Hall.

Sutherland's Streets

Sutherland's streets
have never deserved clearance.
His cottage hospital
where I was safely born
is still well-laundered,
his local library
and respected Institute,
a sore thumb three stories grand,
whose art-school windows
shimmer above
the banded brick
and handsome
terra-cotta frieze
of busy potters,
all of it symmetrical,
confident, Pevsnered.

Here my father took me
one Saturday afternoon
to get my first library card
and thereby started something:
thank you Gilbert Dalton,
A. Stephen Tring, Richmal Crompton,
and thank you
for the hush, the polish
and all the pages turned.

Hearth

I learned to make the fire
in our grate,
newspaper, sticks,
coal-pieces smaller
than my hand
and as the yellow flame
took hold
larger pieces laid
so as to leave
the passages for draught
until our little hearth
could cast out
warmth enough
to last the evening through,
banking it with slack
so its slower burn
would leave some heat
about the room
for morning.
And so in every house like this,
thankful for coal's precious shine,
its smoke of welcome,
habitation, life.

*

This was the time we knew
the glaucous character
of phlegm,
the smoke's particulate sludge,
hawked up and blown
expertly at a sullen coal,

the stuff of dust disease
drooling from old men's
lips as they stop to lean against a wall.
And still
the lazy smoke
and gentle heat rises
through cooling towers,
furnaces and flues
to coddle the planet
in its fatal shawl.

TRIP ADVISOR AND THE DIGLAKE DISASTER

For William Cooke

Field and copse,
genteel English greenery
the roots still feeling their way through
the last shreds of motte and bailey.
The top tip for things to do hereabouts
is the multi-coloured climbing-wall,
or a brass-rubbing of the warrior boss.

Not much-remarked
the 'nearly 80', or 83, or 73 –
78 names are on the stone
though one is chiselled twice,
so 77 though only 3 are buried here
in the Wesleyan churchyard.
The rest lie somehow,
chambered inside the softened land:
19 in the new ten foot,
40 in the East seven foot,
12 in the West eight foot,
and the boy Alfred Hodgkinson,
on his own,
perhaps by the Gauge Door.

EMPIRE NEWS

'What rogues the English are!'
    Naguib Mahfouz, *Palace Walk*

Ocean Island

HMS *Ocean*, touring the Southern Seas, happened by in 1800
        and Banaba, though just a speck at 6 square kilometres and
        barely worth the Empire's tallying, became Ocean Island.

Until 1900 when the chemists found phosphate, soon super-phosphate
        and the British Phosphate Commission risked £50
        on a nine hundred year lease and fertilised Australia till 1979.

By then the Banabans had had to leave their scraped-out isle
        for somewhere near to Fiji some 2000k away.
        A few still dream of a return to their sacred caves
        but with the topsoil gone, the island stripped and lowered towards flood
        what could otherwise be done, to what could they return?

The commissioners left only their mildewed swimming pool,
        their dead machines and did not re-plant a single tree.

The London court allowed a 'moral debt' was owed.

The Bedford Downs Massacre

'Shooting time is all done with in the Kimberley,
      he can have a life here in the cattle.
      His name Goo-woo-something unpronounceable,
      he'll not need that, I'll call him Paddy after me.
And for his other name, for the books,
      why not Bedford, he is a lad from hereabouts,
the hilly pasture, much like Dunstable back home.
And to give him another bit of English
      he could learn to drive the truck,
      the old two-ton Bedford barrelling
      down the roadway, a real Luton bloke.'

             ~

And so he was for sixty years, a stockman
      tinkerer and roadman at Bedford Downs
      where the cattle trod and trod, packing
      and pressing the ground till nothing grew there,
      the emu, bush turkey, cockatoo
      even the rainbow-serpent just roadkill.

             ~

Paddy made this, 'The Bedford Downs Massacre',
      and it is a painting not a story,
      the deep red is all it is, 'the hand of art'
      representing nothing.   *Terra nullius.*

A story is in time, a history, the Bedford Downs Massacre 1921
      for us is a history and it passes.
      For Paddy there is no time, it is not a history.
      It is here, stationary, in his mind and in the paint.

Suez

De Lesseps and his million men did the spadework
        and then it was up to us. As when:

the imperial pigeon-shooters set off
        yet another incident and the natives just don't see
        that this is sport, only sport, why do they make such a fuss
        over a pigeon-pie?
So we have to hang this Egyptian lad in front of his own house,
        and his own mother,
        and take the lash to a good many more.
It will be long remembered.

And so it was.
Though fat Farouk in his fez was at least a pal we could recognise,
        Big-Nose harboured such things.
        He had his snout in the cut from the start and it was lost
        and all our khaki sands were through the glass and gone.

A Respectable Life (notes for an obituary)

Henry, a decent English gent. for sure,
      all the way from his knickerbockers
      in the 1840s to 1923, a safe M.P.,
      Chancellor of the Duchy for a year in 1885,
      always a man of neckties, monocles and means.
Jilted in 1855 (she ran out the back of Marshall and Snelgrove
      into a carriage and her lover's arms), he married Lady Florence,
      but never again after she died in her third childbed.
      Perhaps it was a grief he never could assuage,
      or possibly, because he had sons in hand,
      he had no further need to bother.
It was this Henry gave his name to our not-quite-arterial,
      far from imperial Chaplin Road, our way to the Alhambra,
      Storm over the Nile, Gunga Din, the better man
      unrecognised in our fellow-citizens
      who have made Dr. Heslin's sturdy house a serviceable mosque.
      Was that an accommodation Henry could have sought?
To summarise:
      Henry Chaplin, unexceptionable parliamentary commoner
      of our commonweal, faithful widower, owner
      of a Derby winner, eventual Viscount,
      banked all his life the steady dole of reparation

      won for his career and comfort by his father, the Reverend Henry,
      ex-owner of a far-off family of Grenadan slaves.

'The Company-State'

Did Lady Clive's ferret wear its diamond collar
          when set at large in Shropshire warrens
          or was it too much of a pensioner by then
          for country sports, lank and slack
          on its cushions, fed on caramels?

Leadenhall Street may have looked askance,
          thinking only their grey ledgers
          were the proper instruments of wealth
          but what's the difference after all?
          However austere *seth, shaff* and counting-house
          they all dealt in loot, loot, loot.

Milord Vulture, Diamond Pitt, building docklands
          buying boroughs, 'shaking the pagoda tree'
          down the generations, ancestral easements
          school fees, little luxuries stashed from afar.

The mahout tumbled to the ground however caparisoned.
The sepoy learned to keep his powder dry.

The Empress of India

Queen Victoria does not look too comfortable
      in her cartoon howdah. The elephant
      looks knowing, the mahout, if not mutinous,
      is at best impassive, the scotch bonnet all eyes.
And the queen is feeling the lurch and is holding on.
      For all our efforts Indians will not yet
      become Englishmen and perhaps they never will.

In the Durbar Room at Osborne House sits a statue of
      Ganesh, popular god who likes sweets
      and is said to move whatever gets in the way.
      At his foot sits an obedient rat,
      tail neatly curled, waiting for permission
      to satisfy his undoubted appetite.
      He is the type of continence, governance
      of desire – in fact he could be English!
      He understands that famine, like our rule, is Providence.

That we have not taught their own god's commandment well
      makes us half ashamed.

The Kenya Emergency

'Yes, Mr Howlands was coming to enjoy his work.'
Ngũgĩ Wa Thiong'o, *Weep Not Child*

What is Emergency? Is it inhuman deeds?
       Many wonderful tortures? Where does
       custration come from? Is that the democratic law?
       Is this the British system or the Nazi system?

Castration with barbed wire? Surely not sir,
       not our kind of thing at all. Not even for the Mau Mau.
       Stout gloves and pliers maybe,
       our man on the spot knows the situation best.
       We are driven close but not near to sin.
       Our civilising mission: MMBA, miles and miles of bloody Africa.

St Paddy's Day

'weasels fighting in a hole' to quote-unquote one of their very own,
        some bard or other, and that's how we Britishers see the Irish plain:
        1798 scrabbling after the French; Fenian bombs and bastards;
        Black and Tans; Enniskillen; Warrenpoint;
        Ballymurphy, poor drear Armagh and its murder mile;
        the fancy butchers of the Shankill Road.

But there is Gaelic Guinness and the *craic*,
        horses, jockeys, Irish jokes and squeezebox singalongs,
        St Paddy's Day when Brit expats in Singapore wear
        stovepipe hats in emerald green
        and drunk as leprechauns toast some great-grandad
        who may have hailed from Connemara long ago.

A touch of Irish license once a year's our due,
        we who ever since the Anglo-Normans, Strongbow
        and Mountjoy, Cromwell and his crew have fought
        to bring some tidiness and industry to
        these 'barbarous wretches' and their crackpot land.

It's ours, a British isle we'll not surrender,
        unless, that is, it proves more trouble than it's worth
        and they vote to leave us and sink beneath the waves.
By Jove we'll drink to that we will.

COVERDALE

From a train, as so often noticed, the backside of the city:
Dead motors, fly-tips, tyre-dumps, unclaimed rubble,
       sunless repair shops, any old iron.
Amid this, its grass surrounds striving to stay spruce,
       the Coverdale Baptist Church, eccentric in Ardwick,
       built to be different in 1970, Ernest Geoffrey Seddon,
       architect, now part of Eddie's twentieth century;
Good, careful brick and plentiful glass built to promulgate
       the ghostly psalms.

How amiable are thy dwellings thou Lord of Hosts!
Yea, the sparrow hath found her an house and the swallow
       a nest where she may lay her young

~

Nothing amiable in the end about Fort Ardwick, or Fort
       Beswick, nor any of Hulme's royal crescents,
       the 70s systems built to solve the problem of the poor.
Their old lavatories down the yard (that fearful drop), fitful
       gas mantles, cold clinker in the hearth of a morning,
All that needed clearing and how different, how systematic
       this all looked,
Pueblos of progress but soon leaking, crumbling,
       so much shoddy.
And the poor were spilt there.

And the systemisers were confounded:

God thou knoweth my simpleness, and my faults are not
       hid from thee.

Let not them that trust in thee, O Lord God of Hosts be
      ashamed for my cause...
  for thy sake I have suffered reproof; shame hath
      covered my face...

(This time they/we are trying to do better.)

~

But Coverdale's church, the plaque to the Glory of God
      hidden by weed-stalks,
stands undefeated: drums, vocals and bass guitar are lifted up;
volunteered furniture fills the nave, a clutter of dressers,
      beds, settees and chairs, no doubt other stuff, a kettle
            pots and pans,
each re-claimed, re-made, re-purposed.
And reaching across the kitchen-counter and trestle-tables,
      the cooks, the servers, outside the gardener, the sweepers-up
      and here too the totters-up making the ends meet.

These shall not be defeated.
Not by the girl shooting up into her eyeball,
      not by half-taught plutocrats,
      not by the shit-stained drunk,
      not by the hedge-fund pensionaries,
      not by the battered, not even by the batterer,
      not by all those enjoying their desserts,
      not by she who cannot care,
      not by the comfortable like yours truly.

For the poor shall not always be forgotten; the patient
      abiding of the meek shall not perish for ever.

ANTIQUE CAMELIAS

How much my mother
would have loved
these strange flowers,
their rich petals,
their decorous pink,
though there were none
in our garden,
only aubretia
modestly satisfied,
roses bought by post,
pansies, gawky lupins
shaking themselves.

At one time
there were brambles,
gooseberries, thistles
and dock, hiding-places,
though that space was not ours
until it was bought
so rental garages
would not be built
too close.

Down to the line-post
the garden was for
Monday drying,
sheets and shirts,
the smell and steam,
soap and starch,
the corrugated tub,
the wooden dollypeg –

domestic security,
nothing bought from afar.

My mother and father
came from yards
not gardens,
yards with a lav.
like a brick sentry-box,
cold, newspaper
on a nail,
all to be left behind,
a garden was better
even if the soil
was gravelly,
nasturtiums
making their way through cinders,
but a lawn
was grass
sometimes to be
sat out on,
a deckchair
another new thing
like the mower
so carefully
and regularly oiled.

All this a prospect
from the scullery
and from the table
every day.

MUG AND JUG

a self-portrait without a face
just his blue trousers, white shirt
and tooth-mug

an empty table-cloth, blood-red,
fills the room, I repeat, blood-red and
fills the room

a red boat melting on the water

a man suddenly falling over

shaded silence: enamel plates,
a tall jug

out of some things that can be listed:
sacking, iron, plastic, tar,
cellotex, scrap, often partly burnt

these are of sufficient interest

sadly I want them to lead me elsewhere

BACON'S DOG

anxious or angry
turning and turning
perhaps on a swatch of lawn
its fierce snout pointed at the ground
its teeth glaring but useless
this dog is suffering somehow

cars pass by on the roadway,
beyond that is the line of the sea
then an unhelpful sky

TWO PIANOS

i.m. Roy Fisher

I am listening to Renato Sellani (piano)
who has the softest touch,
sometimes so close to silence.
Sellani at lunchtime, the gnome
of 'My Funny Valentine',
the sun strong through the window,
his cigarette smoke hanging in its light.

And I am put in mind of an old friend
confined to his chair, looking at
Earl Sterndale in the mirror above his mantelpiece.
He can see enough from there he says.
He paid attention.

The thing about them both is the piano,
for Roy that and poetry,
the codes of rhythm.
To their innermost of course I was not privy.

DID I REALLY DO THIS?

All my life I have insisted
that I really did walk out of school
on my very first day, my very first morning.

Yes, it is true.   I just left the classroom
when the teacher's back was turned
and walked out and home,

three-quarters of a mile across a road
admittedly less busy than it is now
to reach our street and arrive

at the top of our path and see my mother
look up astonished from the kitchen step
she was scrubbing clean on hands and knees.

I had looked forward to the nursery sandpit,
its lorries, tipper-trucks and cars
but they had moved me next door to desks and sums.

In the afternoon I was reconciled:
I did not want a smock and a baby-sleep
but to join the world: pullovers and pencils.

All true, I insist, and how well I remember
most of it, though what does it mean,
does it belong in the story I have to tell?

PERCE

Perce!   Hey Perce!   Wait!

I've been trying to catch you all my life!
Wait a minute.
I'd just like a word.

You'll not know me
but I'm your nephew
I was here before you were gone,
you wouldn't know.
I'm your replacement sort of.

Look, I'll be quick.
It's a good photo that you left,
smart, smiling, hair nicely combed,
you look friendly,
was that you?
that sort of lad?

All my life I've tried to catch you.

Don't be a stranger

or this ghost.
I've had to make you up
from the photograph
and having your name,
still laughable Percy,
and here you are –
you might pause and look at me
and wonder who –

'what's this lad want of me?'

But you must get on,
your greatcoat's gone
and now in your tropical kit,
you've got your death to deal with.

You turn away
back into the photograph –
I couldn't replace you
for all the years I've had,
and you weren't born to be a memory.

Why should you stop,
look over your shoulder even?
You're there now
and I've nothing for you.

THE SHADES

they look up
for a moment
their attention drawn
and nod and note

that their niece
has followed them
just this afternoon
—how could that be
how could it be her time?

but they know just how
and that it is

they are not much occupied
no sweeping
nothing novel
no surprise

their footprints
do not stray far
their hems and
trouser cuffs
trail in the dust
dried nosegays
no more than sticks
are shuffled
from one hand
to another

they have nothing to say

they do not wish
or watch
or wait or greet
the boulder is neither
shelter nor feature

she takes her place
a small way off

the most they do
is know

THE WINDOW AGAIN

How often do I come to this window?
Outside, on a step at eye-level, a hefty
long-lived pot-plant, its leathery leaves
doing their best against autumn.
Behind that, tidy brickwork, its mortar now going
black in places, though only slowly
and with what looks like
some beginnings of moss.
This wall cuts out of sight all but some branches
and foliage of the confident trees beyond,
another year – leaves
and bare branches, their regular cycle.
To the left, in the right-angle of the window-frame
a clear patch of sky, just now a thin grey
that continues through the shifting gaps in the branches.
And that's it, as much as there is to be seen,
parts of things.   At night I draw the blind.

INTERVAL

Did you just give up and go,
decide that seventy-odd was fair-dos
and anyway you'd had enough
of pills, scans and what you can't remember?

All that stuff in envelopes and biscuit tins,
photos that deserved another look
will have to take their chances now,
you couldn't deal with everything.

May those of us most likely to be missing you
get past that and live our life.
You won't want to spoil one day of what's
left to us since we were pushed out here
into this interval that always ends
before it's finished but has to do.

HERE I GO

Here I go, no, not 'here I go again',
but here I go the once, the only time,
the approaching final second, that moment,
no other, no second chance as
inside this boundary there is less and less
able to marshal its chemistry
against this change,
less and less of this life
that only knows that it is life that it wants,
life that it wants.

ACKNOWLEDGEMENTS

Some of these poems have appeared in *The Manchester Review, Moving Worlds, PN Review, Poetry and Audience, Raceme, Stand,* and in an on-line poetry anthology at Manchester Metropolitan University.   Many thanks for criticism and encouragement to my editors Michael Schmidt and John McAuliffe and to all at Carcanet as well as Jon Glover, Robert Gray, J.J. Healy, Alf Louvre, Judith Wainwright and John Whale.   'Here on Earth' is dedicated to the memory of my friend Adolfo Trippini.